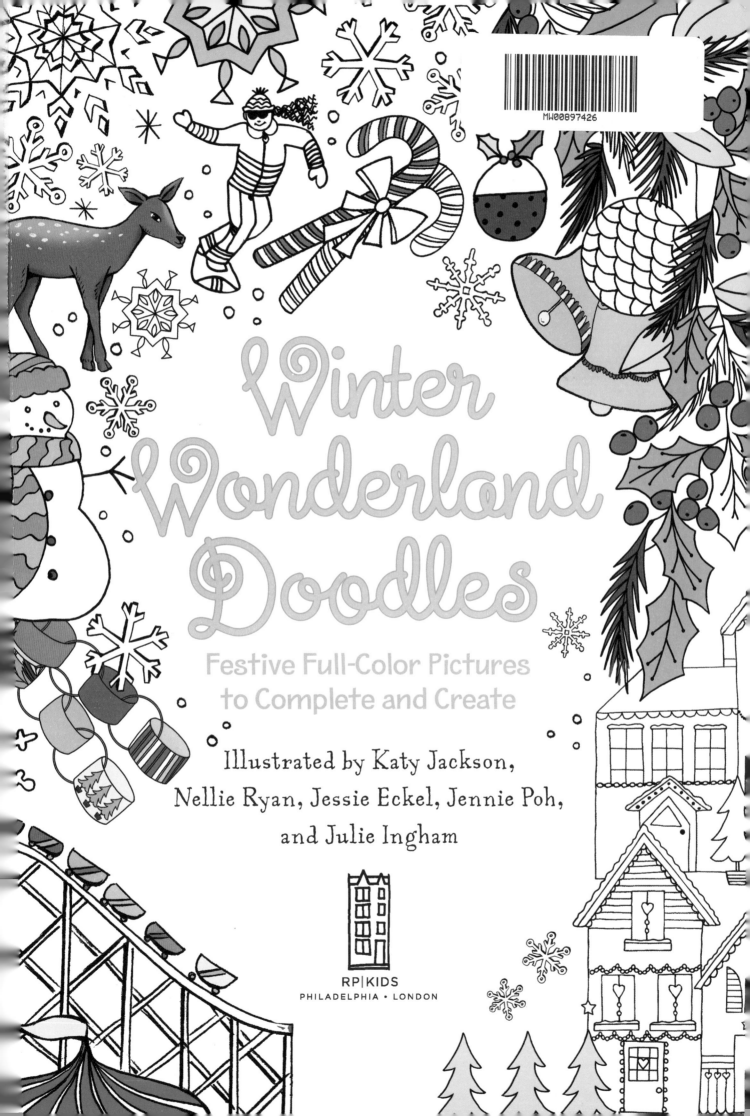

Winter Wonderland Doodles

Festive Full-Color Pictures to Complete and Create

Illustrated by Katy Jackson,
Nellie Ryan, Jessie Eckel, Jennie Poh,
and Julie Ingham

RP|KIDS
PHILADELPHIA • LONDON

It's time to get creative!

Doodle delightful designs and color with confidence
as you complete this wonderful, wintry book
in your own unique way.

Whether you're drawing detail with a black pen or
adding vibrant color with markers, pencils, or crayons,
it's up to you to add your signature style to every picture.

If you are drawing on top of colored areas on the pages,
leave your ink to dry for a moment to avoid smudges.

Now go wild and get inspired!

Books published by Running Press are available at special discounts for bulk purchases in the United States by corporations, institutions, and other organizations. For more information, please contact the Special Markets Department at the Perseus Books Group, 2300 Chestnut Street, Suite 200, Philadelphia, PA 19103, or call (800) 810-4145, ext. 5000, or e-mail special.markets@perseusbooks.com.

ISBN 978-0-7624-4675-9

9 8 7 6 5 4 3
Digit on the right indicates the number of this printing

Illustrated by Katy Jackson, Nellie Ryan, Jessie Eckel, Jennie Poh, and Julie Ingham
Edited by Jen Wainwright
Cover design by Angie Allison
Interior design by Zoe Quayle

This edition published by:
Running Press Kids
An Imprint of Running Press Book Publishers
A Member of the Perseus Books Group
2300 Chestnut Street
Philadelphia, PA 19103–4371

Visit us on the web!
www.runningpress.com/kids

This book was
created, completed,
and colored by

Stella D.

Complete the cute candy canes.

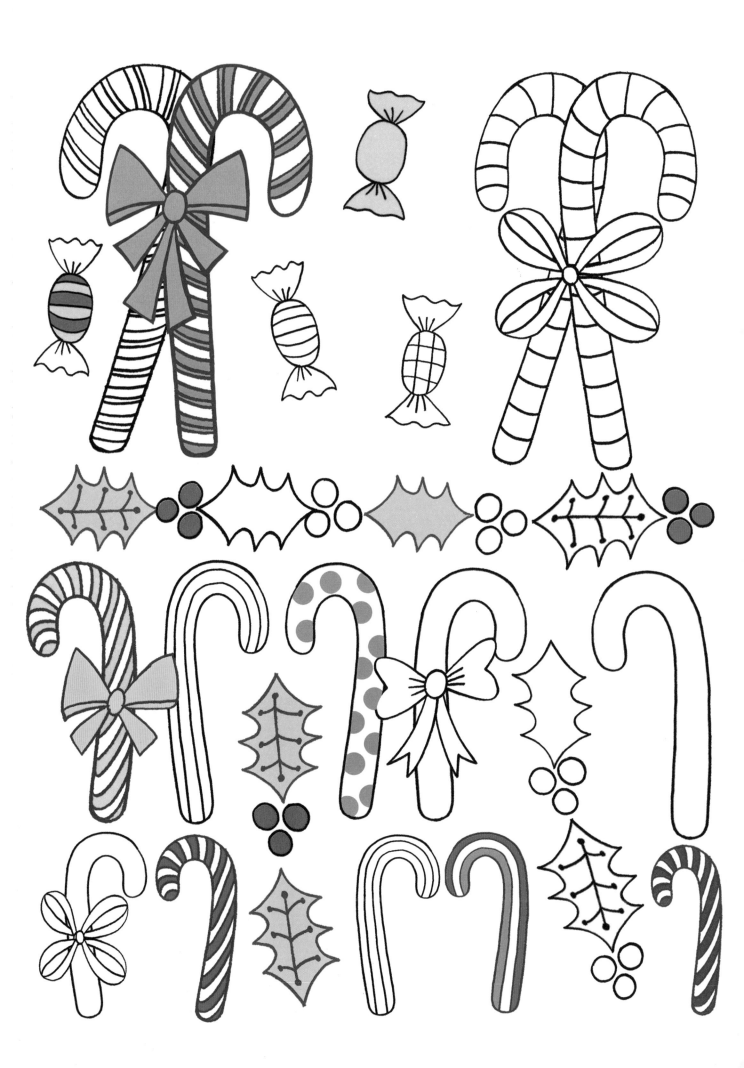

Woolly but wonderful. Decorate the winter sweaters.

Finish the festive gift wrap.

Give the ice skaters glittering costumes.

Cover the page in holly and ivy.

Create and decorate more Christmas cookies.

Decorate the tiles around the roaring fire.

Add more sparkling snowflakes and stars.

Finish the rainbow and add more prancing reindeer.

Decorate the angels' wings.

Decorate the ornaments.

Fill the sky with twinkling stars.

Finish the ice queen's dress, and complete her frozen kingdom.

Complete the pretty patchwork quilt.

Finish the gorgeous dresses for the Christmas party.

Snowmen or penguins?

Party!

What beautiful Christmas presents ...

Design the ultimate winter coat.

Fill the tree with robins and owls.

Finish the fairground at the Winter Wonderland.

Design your own cute Christmas cards.

Cover the page with bright bows and ribbons.

Count down to Christmas.

Complete the Advent calendar.

Add more trees to the snowy forest.

Finish the mugs of delicious hot chocolate.

Who else is zooming down the mountain?

Ring out the bells for Christmas Day!

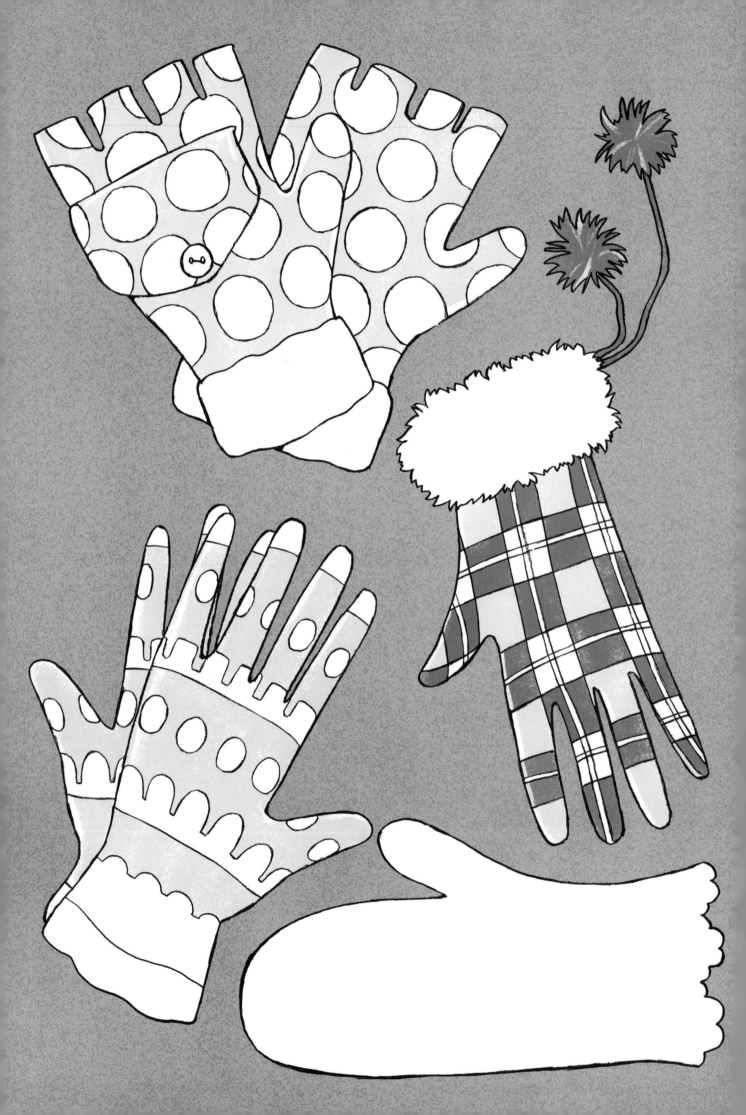

Complete the warm winter wear.

Complete the colorful fireworks.

Fill the winter wonderland with lights and twinkling trees.

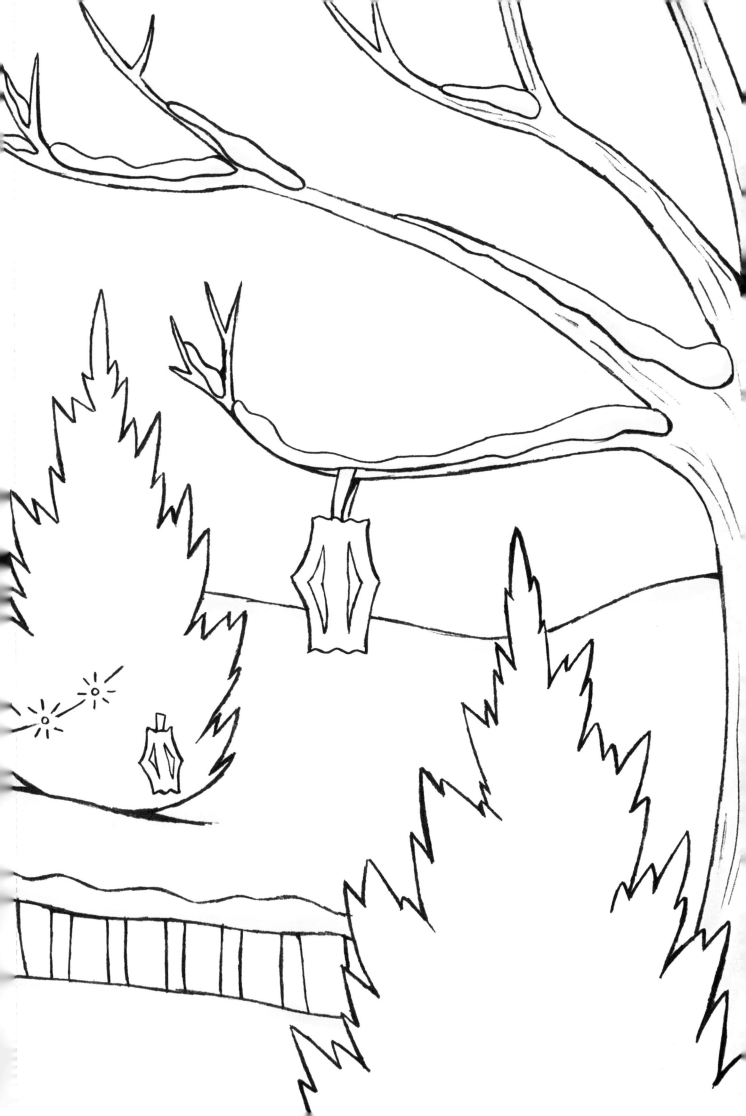

Make these gift tags terrific.

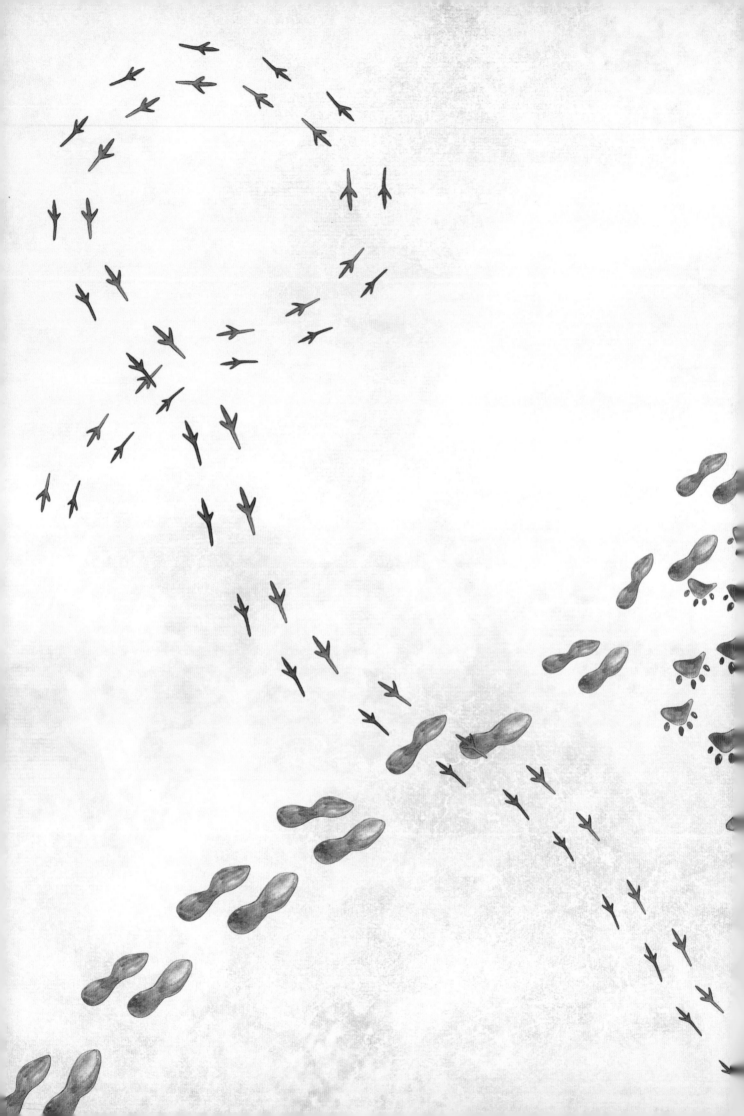

Make more footprints in the snow.

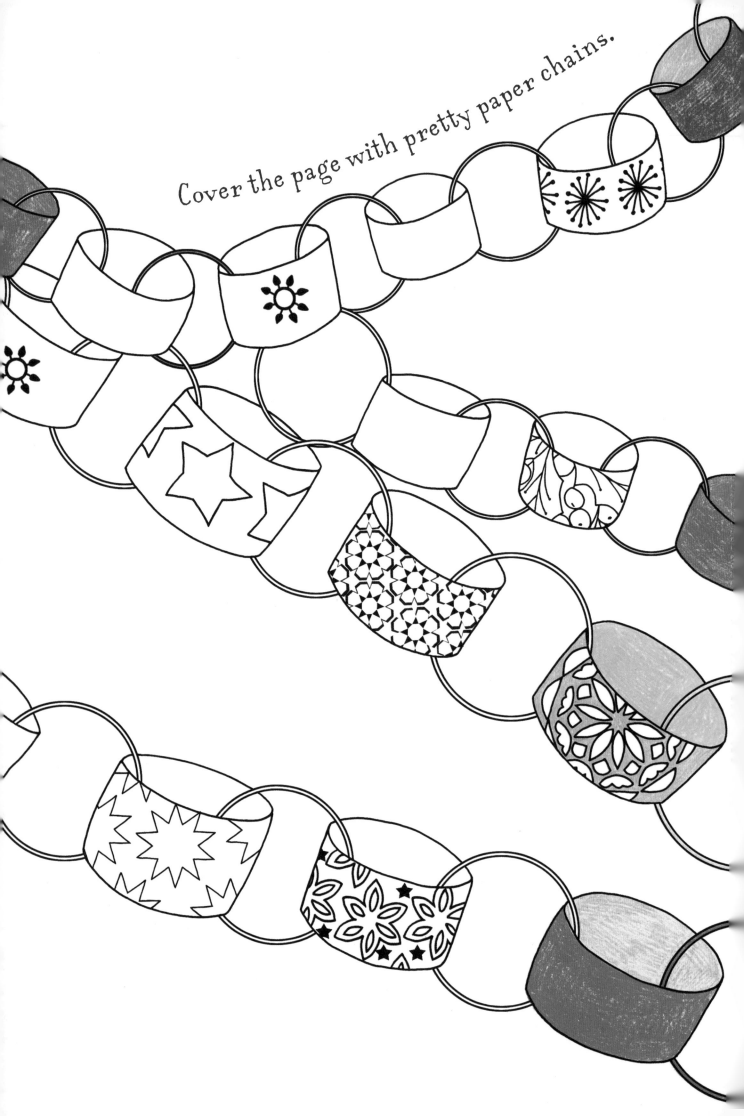

Cover the page with pretty paper chains.

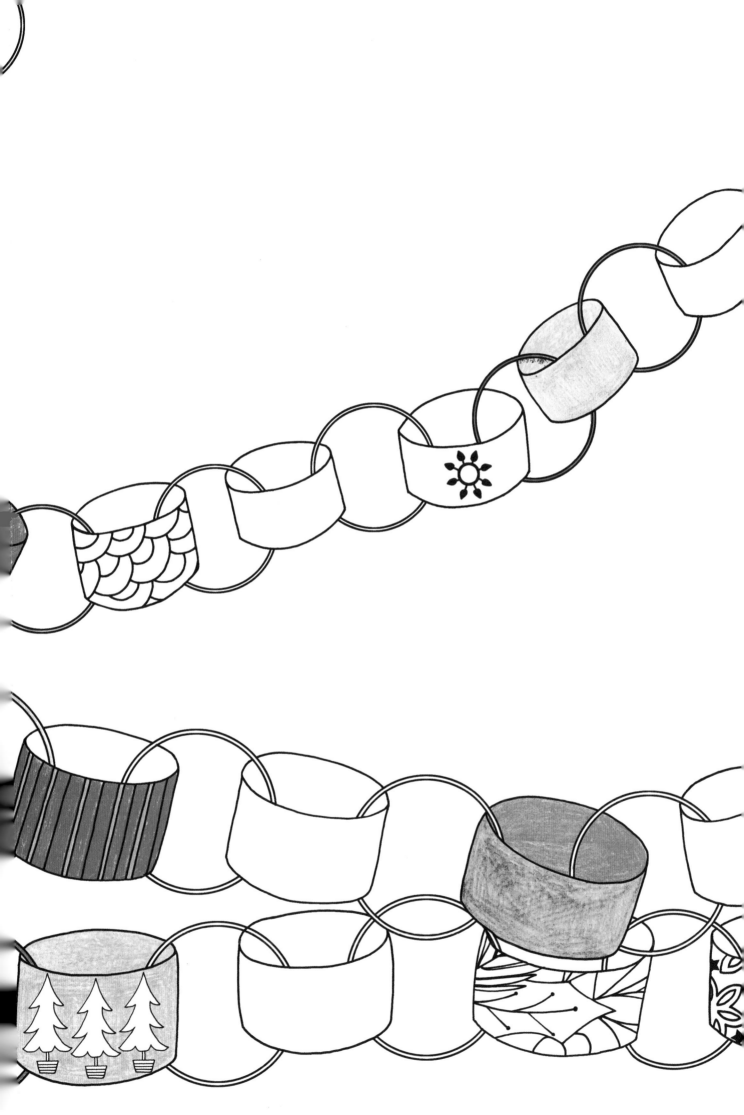

Finish the Eskimos' warm winter outfit.

Yum! Bake and ice more Christmas cupcakes.

Fill the snowy woodland.

Make cold days better with beautiful blankets.

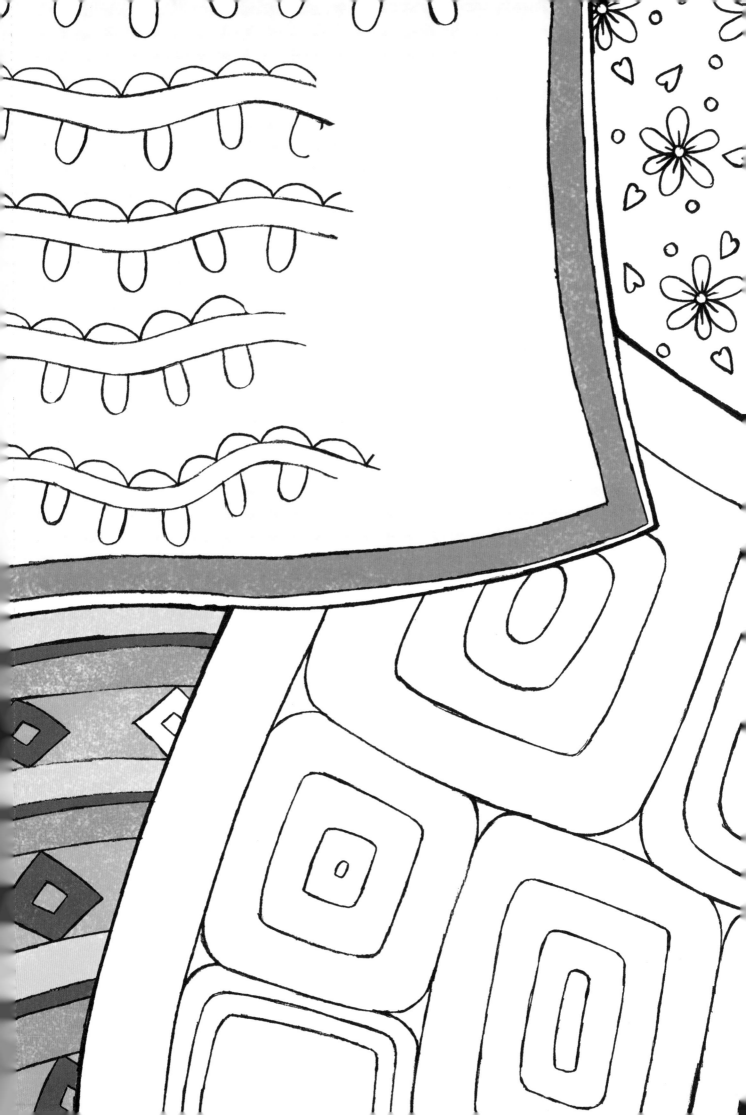

Fiery flames . . .

. . . and frosty flakes.

Fill the street with bright and festive houses.

Complete the tasty puddings.

Add more cozy igloos to the icy North.

Design more snuggly scarves.

Help Jack Frost to make more icy patterns.

Fill the Christmas market with festive treats.

Decorate the stockings hanging by the fire.

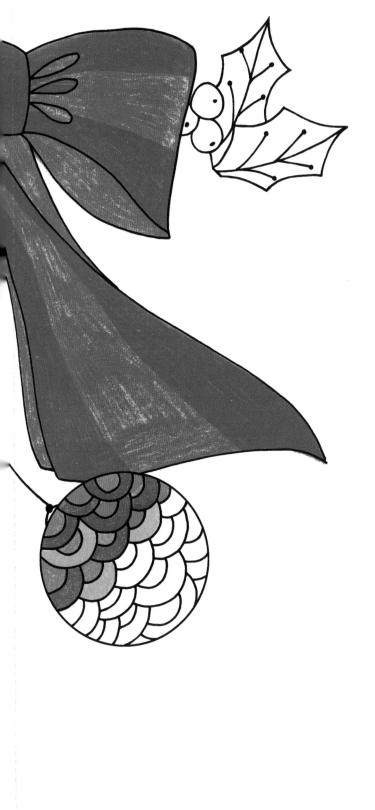

Complete the wreath to hang on the front door.

What else have Santa's elves made?

What's in the snow globes?

Give the trees more twisty branches.

Cover the page with Christmas flowers.

Complete the cool caps and hip hats.

Add more buildings and bridges to the Japanese garden.

Decorate the trees with beautiful ornaments.

Finish the incredible, edible gingerbread house.

Pile Santa's sleigh high with presents,
and finish the snowy scene.

Complete the costumes at the ballet.

Fill the frames with wintry pictures ...

...and surround them with twinkly Christmas lights.

Complete the sparkling ice palace.

What's in the snowy garden?

Complete the Christmas window displays.

Cozy nights by candlelight.

Ring in the New Year in style with balloons and streamers.

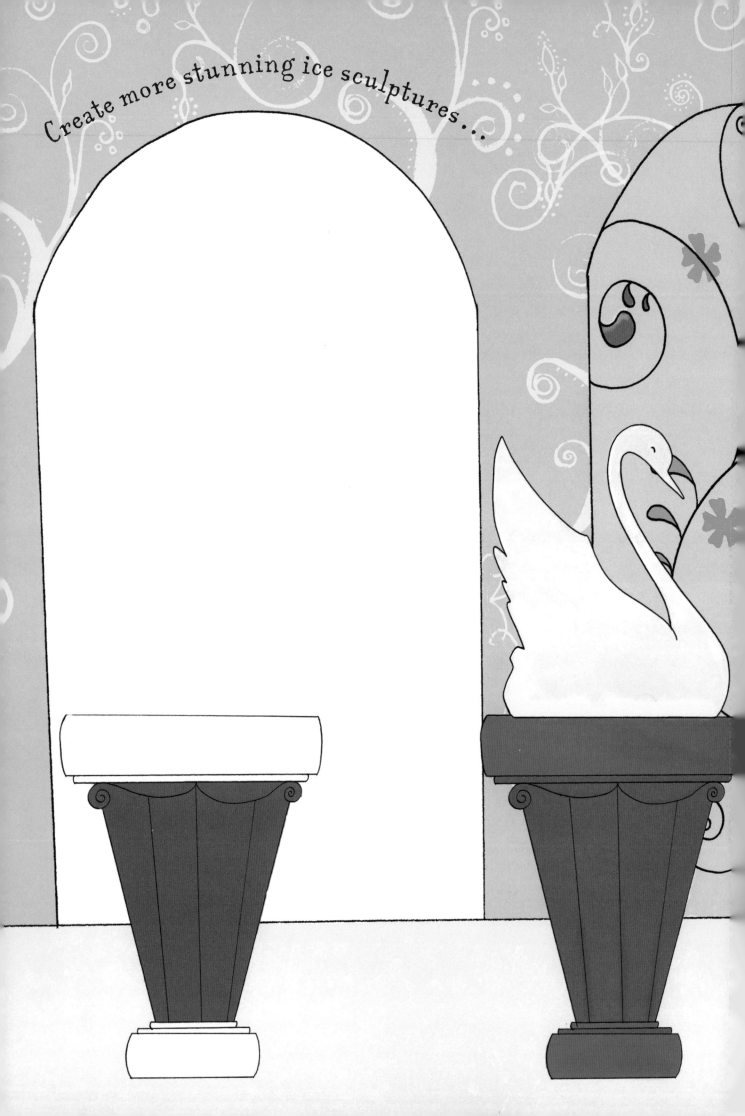

Create more stunning ice sculptures...

...and decorate the arches.

Finish the strings of Christmas lights.

Add more flowers poking
through the snow.

Finish the roofs for Santa to fly over.